Biomes

by Ruth Owen

Consultant: Jordan Stoleru
Science Educator

BEARPORT
PUBLISHING

Minneapolis, Minnesota

Conter

Credits

Cover and title page, © Jillian/Adobe Stock, © Rixie/Adobe Stock, © Ivelina/Adobe Stock, © jimcumming88/Adobe Stock, © KenCanning/iStock, © cinoby/iStock, and © Dgwildlife/iStock; 5A, © Romolo Tavani/Shutterstock; 5B, © Lex0077/Shutterstock; 5C, © Andrei Stepanov/Shutterstock; 5D, © Deliris/Shutterstock; 7, © Dmitry Pichugin/Shutterstock; 9, © Imagentle/Shutterstock; 10–11, © Solarisys/Shutterstock; 13, © Angelika Smile/Shutterstock; 15T, © Richard Whitcombe/Shutterstock; 15M, © GagliardiPhotography/Shutterstock; 15B, © Mario Krpan/Shutterstock; 16–17, © Jessica A Robinson/Shutterstock; 18–19, © Dago Martinez/Shutterstock; 19, © Evgeny Haritonov/Shutterstock; 20–21, © Yegor Larin/Shutterstock; 21 © Ksenya_89/Shutterstock; 22–23, © Tunatura/Shutterstock; 25, © Piyaset/Shutterstock; 27A, © Curioso.Photography/Shutterstock; 27B, © Sergei Mishchenko/Shutterstock; 27C, © Repina Valeriya/Shutterstock; 27D, © Yegor Larin/Shutterstock; 27E, © Kichigin/Shutterstock; 28A, © Rubeus Olivander/Shutterstock; 28B, © Polarpx/Shutterstock; 28C, © SergeUWPhoto/Shutterstock; 28D, © Sergei Mishchenko/Shutterstock; and 28E, © geogif/Shutterstock.

Bearport Publishing Company Product Development Team

President: Jen Jenson; Director of Product Development: Spencer Brinker; Managing Editor: Allison Juda; Associate Editor: Naomi Reich; Associate Editor: Tiana Tran; Senior Designer: Colin O'Dea; Associate Designer: Elena Klinkner; Associate Designer: Kayla Eggert; Product Development Specialist: Anita Stasson

Library of Congress Cataloging-in-Publication Data is available at www.loc.gov or upon request from the publisher.

ISBN: 979-8-88822-039-9 (hardcover)
ISBN: 979-8-88822-231-7 (paperback)
ISBN: 979-8-88822-354-3 (ebook)

For more information, write to Bearport Publishing, 5357 Penn Avenue South, Minneapolis, MN 55419.

Earth's Beautiful Biomes

Earth is covered in big oceans with whales under the waves. There are huge **forests** full of furry creatures. Cold, icy **tundra** and hot **deserts** have less life.

Scientists sort the different major types of natural communities on Earth into groups. Those groups are called **biomes**.

Many scientists say there are five major biome types. However, some make more specific groups. If broken up this way, there are up to 11 kinds of places on Earth.

Sun, Soil, Rocks, and Rain

How do we sort biomes? They are made up of both living and non-living things. Non-living parts of a biome include the type of land. Does a place have dirt, rocks, or sand? Are there rivers or streams? Is it covered in mountains or valleys?

Different types of biomes can share some things in common. There might be two places with soil and flat lands. However, all of the things in an area add up to what type of biome it is.

An area's **climate** is another factor. This is the expected weather in an area. The kinds of seasons in a place are part of its climate. So is the typical temperature during those times. The amount of **precipitation** each year is an important part of climate.

Weather is what happens from day to day. There is rainy, warm, or windy weather. The climate describes an area's usual weather over many years. That means one day with odd weather does not change a place's climate.

What Lives Here?

Land and climate alone do not make up a biome. The biome also includes the living things in the area.

Often, the plants and animals in a biome are **adapted** to where they live. The life is fit for the land and climate.

Biomes are sometimes thought of as life zones. That's because each kind of biome is best for certain living things. In fact, *bio* means life.

It's Easy Being Green

Some areas on Earth have many trees. These are forest biomes. Much of the land on Earth is covered with forests. However, forests aren't all the same.

There are a few kinds of forests. Each kind has a different land and climate. The different forests may have different plants and animals, too.

The thing all forest biomes share in common is that they have many trees. Because there are many other differences, some scientists break up kinds of forests into different biomes.

Tropical forests are warm and get a lot of rain. Their trees are often large and leafy. Most of the time, the temperatures in boreal (BOR-ee-uhl) forests are below freezing. Trees in these forests usually have needle-like leaves. Temperate (TEM-pur-it) forests are in areas with warm and cold seasons. They have a mix of tree types.

Tropical forests are near the equator. Boreal forests are in more northern regions. Temperate forests are between. They are north of tropical forests and south of boreal forests.

A tropical forest

A boreal forest

A temperate forest

A Grassy Wonderland

Unlike forest biomes, **grasslands** don't have trees. Instead, the land is covered with low-growing plants, including many grasses. These biomes have a dry climate. There is just enough rain to help the grasses grow. Large groups of plant-eating animals live there. They graze on, or eat, the plants.

Savannas are a type of grassland. They have just a few trees dotted around. Savannas have two seasons. One is dry with very little or no rain. The other has lots of precipitation.

Living without Water

Desert biomes are some of the driest places on Earth. In most deserts, hardly any rain falls. Most deserts are hot during the day all year round. Because of this harsh climate, deserts have fewer plants and animals.

Desert plants have learned how to live with little rainfall. Many animals there stay in cool, underground homes during the day. They come out at night to find food.

Tundra biomes are also very dry. However, they are cold almost all the time. Flat tundra land is covered with a thin layer of soil. Below this, the ground is frozen. Trees cannot push their roots into the icy ground. Only low-growing plants can live in these biomes.

Tundra are mostly covered by snow. It melts for only a short time. This is when plants bloom. Some tundra plants grow, flower, and make seeds for just a couple of months out of the year.

Blue Biomes

About 71 percent of Earth is covered with water. These areas are **aquatic** (uh-KWAT-ik) biomes.

Most of these biomes are part of the oceans. The water in ocean biomes has salt. It is home to water-loving plants and thousands of different animals.

Earth also has many freshwater biomes. Rivers, streams, ponds, and lakes are all kinds of these biomes. Their waters are not salty like the oceans. However, they are still full of plant and animal life.

Land and Life at Risk

Plants and animals usually do best in one type of biome. But many biomes all over the planet are changing. **Climate change** is causing rising temperatures. Rain and snowfall are being affected, too. This can put a whole biome at risk. Some biomes have already been changed forever.

The life and land in a biome are connected. If the land changes, the life on it may not be able to live there anymore. Likewise, if certain plants or animals leave, the land will likely change.

Forest and tundra biomes are at the highest risk due to climate change.

Sorting Wild Places

Why sort Earth into biomes in the first place? Grouping similar places makes them easier to study. It also helps us understand our planet better. Two forest biomes may not be near each other. However, their land, climate, animals, and plants may be similar. That's the power of biomes!

Sometimes, plants or animals in a place need help. Scientists are taking lessons from one area to another. They use what they have learned about biomes to help similar areas all over the world.

Mapping Earth's Biomes

Where on Earth can we find different biomes? Let's take a look at the major biomes around the world!

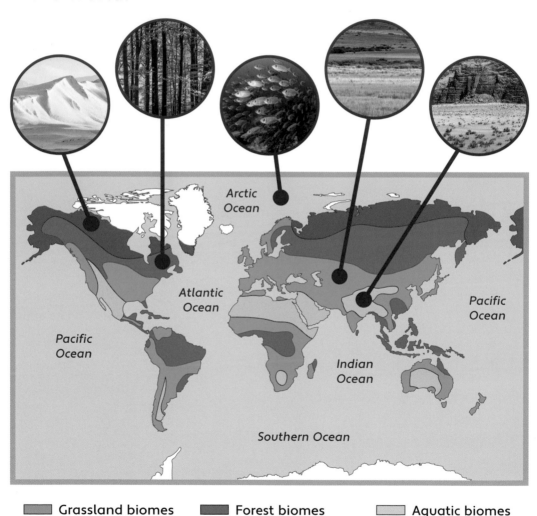

Arctic Ocean

Atlantic Ocean

Pacific Ocean

Pacific Ocean

Indian Ocean

Southern Ocean

Grassland biomes

Desert biomes

Forest biomes

Tundra biomes

Aquatic biomes

★ SilverTips for REVIEW

Review what you've learned. Use the text to help you.

Define key terms

adapted   precipitation

biome   seasons

climate

Check for understanding

What kinds of things are included when considering an area's biome?

Compare and contrast two types of biomes.

Why might climate change impact biomes?

Think deeper

Think about the area where you live. What kind of biome do you think you live in?

★ SilverTips on TEST-TAKING

- **Make a study plan.** Ask your teacher what the test is going to cover. Then, set aside time to study a little bit every day.

- **Read all the questions carefully.** Be sure you know what is being asked.

- **Skip any questions** you don't know how to answer right away. Mark them and come back later if you have time.

Glossary

adapted changed over time to be fit for the environment

aquatic having to do with the water

biomes areas where certain kinds of land, climate, and living creatures form natural communities

climate the typical weather in a place

climate change changes to the usual weather patterns around Earth, including the warming of the air and oceans, due to human activities

deserts dry biomes with little rainfall and few plants and animals

forests biomes where many trees grow

grasslands biomes marked by wide, open areas of land with low-growing grasses and plants

precipitation rain, sleet, hail, or snow

tropical having to do with warm areas of Earth near the center of the globe

tundra biomes where the ground is frozen most if not all of the time

Read More

Bergin, Raymond. *Warming Planet (What on Earth? Climate Change Explained).* Minneapolis: Bearport Publishing Company, 2022.

Nargi, Lela. *Forest Biomes (Exploring Biomes).* Minneapolis: Jump!, Inc., 2023.

Simpson, Phillip. *Tundra Biomes around the World (Fact Finders: Exploring Earth's Biomes).* North Mankato, MN: Capstone Press, 2020.

Learn More Online

1. Go to **www.factsurfer.com** or scan the QR code below.

2. Enter "**Biomes**" into the search box.

3. Click on the cover of this book to see a list of websites.

Index

About the Author

Ruth Owen has been writing books for more than 12 years. She lives in Cornwall, England, just minutes from the ocean. Ruth loves to research and write books about nature.